Some Things For Which The South Did Not Fight

In The War Between The States

Henry Tucker Graham, DD, LLD

REPRINTED BY

Wake Forest, NC
www.scuppernongpress.com

Some Things For Which The South Did Not Fight In The War Between The States
By Henry Tucker Graham

Edited by Frank B. Powell, III

©2021 The Scuppernong Press

First Printing

The Scuppernong Press
PO Box 1724
Wake Forest, NC 27588
www.scuppernongpress.com

Cover and book design by Frank B. Powell, III

All rights reserved

Printed in the United States of America

No part of this book may be reproduced or transmitted in any form or by any means, electronic or mechanical, including photocopying, recording, or by any information and storage and retrieval system, without written permission from the editor and/or publisher.

International Standard Book Number
                    ISBN 978-1-942806-35-6

Library of Congress Control Number: 2021941808

Contents

Introduction iii

Foreword v

Some Things For Which The South Did Not Fight 1

I. They did not fight for a Rebellion 3

II. They did not fight to "Destroy the United States" 4

III. It is charged our Fathers fought to maintain slavery 9

IV. History records no more brilliant fight ever made in defense of home and country and constitutional rights than that of the "men who were the gray." 13

Closing 16

About the Author 19

Introduction

We first discovered this little book, a pamphlet really, in a collection of books which were being donated to the UDC. It did not take long to realize how important it was to republish it for today's readers.

Published in 1946, *Some Things For Which The South Did Not Fight* speaks to our society today and the misguided efforts to change and/or erase our history and culture. Everyone, especially young people, should have a copy and read it thoroughly, because the true history of the South and the United States is not being taught in our public schools, colleges and universities. History is history and cannot be changed, but it can be forgotten and we must not let this happen.

Rev. Dr. Henry Tucker Graham is an exceptional author and very well educated. This little book shows his wisdom, research and plain old common sense. We were fascinated by his career as well as his education. But his true calling was to be a pastor and from all accounts he was a great one.

This book has been completely reset in a modern typeface, with light editing for easier reading. A short biography of the author is added along with a few photographs.

With all the falsehoods, mis-truths and out right lies being spread all over our country and the world, we feel *Some Things For Which The South Did Not Fight* is a valuable resource which can be used to help stem the tide of political correctness.

— *Frank B. Powell, III, editor*

Foreword

This pamphlet is dedicated to the Public Schools of North Carolina by the Anson Chapter, United Daughters of the Confederacy, in honor of its author, Dr. Henry Tucker Graham, of Florence, South Carolina.

The author's purpose in preparing this historical treatise was to correct certain prevailing misconceptions concerning the ideals and motives which prompted our Southern leaders to engage our people in a bloody contest of arms with our Northern neighbors, and by a truthful presentation of some generally unknown data, thus remove any stigma which might unjustly have accrued to their memory because of a distortion of certain facts surrounding their participation in the War Between the States.

The author's interest in this subject was intensified by the fact his minister-father was a personal friend of General "Stonewall" Jackson and often entertained the general and his wife in the manse at Winchester, VA.

Dr. Graham, a former president of the Hampden-Sidney College, and for twenty years the beloved pastor of the First Presbyterian Church of Florence, South Carolina, is well qualified for this self-imposed task, both from the standpoint of scholarship and personal integrity. Because of his burning desire to clear the gallant leaders of his beloved Southland of the unjust charge of petty prejudice and political inconsistency, the arduous task of research and investigation necessary for the preparation of a historical paper of this kind has been for the author, a labor of love.

It is not the purpose or desire of the sponsors of this pamphlet to disparage or detract from the character or courage of our Northern neighbors in the waging of that mighty conflict, but believing that the information contained in this little booklet will serve a legitimate purpose in helping to establish certain important facts of history pertinent to the Southern Cause, in connection with the War Between the States, we heartily recommend this brochure as parallel reading in the teaching of history in the public schools of our state.

Joseph Orlando Bowman
May, 1946
Superintendent of Anson County Schools
Wadesboro, NC

Some Things For Which The South Did Not Fight

--- IN THE ---

War Between The States

Out of the first World War there came many things of interest — some tragic, some pathetic, and some comic. I recall one song the Doughboys loved to sing:

"I don't know what this war's about
But you bet, by jinks, I'll soon find out."

I speak largely, if not altogether, to those whose kinsmen wore the gray in the War For Southern Independence. In a vague sort of way you probably think they were "right" — but I am wondering how many of you could give a clear-cut statement of the real causes of that great struggle which ended so disastrously for the South, and thus repel the false charges laid against our Fathers and our section?

I am especially concerned lest these young people, or their children, should some day be led to think of our gallant Fathers as traitors and rebels.

There is grave danger that our school children are learning much more about Massachusetts, than about the Carolinas, and hearing more often of Northern leaders than of the splendid men who led the Southern hosts alike in peace and war.

Not many years ago the high school in an important South Carolina town devoted much time to the celebration of Lincoln's Birthday — while Lee, Jackson, Hampton and George Washington, received no mention. You have all heard of Paul Revere's ride made famous by the skillful pen of a New England writer. He rode seven miles out of Boston, ran into a squadron of British horsemen and was back in a British dungeon before daybreak. But how many of you have heard of Jack Jouitte's successful and daring ride of forty miles from a wayside tavern to Charlottesville to warn Governor Jefferson and the Legislature of the coming of a British squadron bent upon their capture?

You have heard of the Boston Tea Party, but how many know of the Wilmington, North Carolina, Tea Party? At Boston they disguised themselves as Indians and under cover of darkness threw the tea overboard. At Wilmington they did the same thing without disguise in broad daylight.

With the utter disregard of the facts they blandly claim that the Republic was founded at Plymouth Rock, while all informed persons know Plymouth was 13½ years behind the times, and when its Colony was reduced to a handful of half-starved immigrants on the bleak shores of Massachusetts, there was a prosperous Colony of 2,000 people along the James under the sunlit skies of the South.

The fact is New England has been so busy writing history it hasn't had time to make it. While the South has been so busy **making history** it hasn't had time to **write it.**

Hence to correct false impressions I would talk to you about some of the things for which our Fathers did **not fight.**

George Washington

I. They did not fight for a Rebellion. That term was "coined" by demagogues to stir the lagging zeal of the North, and to cast discredit upon the South.

The government itself in publishing the official records of that historic struggle chose this title: *"The Official Records of the War of the Rebellion"* — a title as false as it is misleading. Our Fathers fought for rights which had never been seriously challenged until 1861. Five times before 1861 Massachusetts threatened to secede and there was no talk of an army to force her back into the Union. There was never but one great Rebellion in America, that began in 1775. There was never but one great Rebel — that was George Washington. The government tried to indict Mr. Davis for treason but was forced to abandon the case. They threatened, but did not even dare file charges vs.

General Lee. In his first Inaugural Mr. Lincoln refers to the seceding states and to the threat of hostilities but never speaks of "rebellion." But by March 1864 he has caught the infection now so prevalent in the North and speaks sharply of rebels and rebellion.

II. They did not fight to "Destroy the United States."

The existence of the USA was never for a moment imperiled. Its constituency would have been changed and its boundaries altered, but its destruction was never attempted, or even desired. Whatever the outcome of the war the USA would have still continued to be a great, growing and powerful Republic.

That indeed was one great reason for our failure.

Because the existence of the USA was not even endangered her bonds and notes could always command a market, whereas the value of Confederate Bonds depended wholly upon the success of the South and so in the last twelve or eighteen months of the war it was increasingly difficult to find a purchaser, and without these "sinews of war" defeat became inevitable — for a nation cannot fight very long without money.

Now let us glance at the history of the American Constitution. In May 1787 there met in Independence Hall in Philadelphia (the same Hall in which the Declaration of Independence had been made just eleven years before) the representatives of thirteen free independent Republics to draft a Constitution and so "form a more perfect union" than the loose and ineffective Confederation which then existed. Each State (or Republic) was intensely jealous of its sovereign rights. Rhode Island soon withdrew because it feared that its rights as a small state would not be adequately safeguarded. Later it adopted the Constitution as drawn and amended by the adoption of the Bill of Rights (the first ten amendments) as a part of the instrument. William E. Gladstone, the British Statesman, later declared that our Constitution is "the greatest political document ever drawn by a single body in the history of the world."

When the constitution had been adopted by the requisite number of States, the USA was launched upon the stormy sea of political life with the novel and happy device that populations were represented in the Lower House, while each state, large and small, enjoyed equal representation in the Senate, and thus safe-guarded each state vs. the possible tyranny of numbers.

The Constitution represented a partnership into which each party entered freely, and was equally free to withdraw if it felt that its best interests so demanded.

Did you ever hear of a political or business partnership which could not be dissolved — once a partner always a partner?

The right to secede was not written into the Constitution but was tacitly understood by every member of the Convention, and by their constituents back home. Why write into the document that which no one questioned for a moment? But George Mason, astute and farsighted Statesman that he was, saw the danger which that omission might some day provoke, and voiced it in his shrewd comment: "I see the poison that lurks beneath the eagle's wing."

Had Daniel Webster been present and given voice to the startling view later uttered by him — and often quoted since — that "the USA is an **indissoluble union** of indestructible States" he would have been "laughed out of court," for whoever heard of an "indissoluble partnership?" Or had Abraham Lincoln been present and declared as he later did: "The Union is older than the States" his **sanity** would have been gravely questioned, for that would have been the exact equivalent of claiming this building in which we are gathered is older than the bricks of which it is composed. There must have been separate and individual States before there could be a United States. But the word Secession, though assumed by all, was not written into the Contract of Union, and thereby hangs a tale of "blood and sweat and tears."

Are you aware that President Lincoln in his Inaugural Address (March 4, 1861) made this statement: (Quoting from Republican Platform 1860) "We denounce the lawless invasion by armed force of the soil of any State or Territory, no matter under what pretext, as among the **gravest of crimes.**"

Yet less than six weeks later he called for 75,000 troops to invade the South. Surely, "Consistency, thou art indeed a jewel" rare!

Incidentally this drove Virginia (in April) and North Carolina (in May) out of the Union — and these two states furnished half of the total armed forces of the CSA.

Strangely enough the right to secede was never seriously questioned until after Sumter fell.

Wm. Howard Russell, the brilliant correspondent of the *London Times*, was sent to America early in '61 to give first hand reports on the situation. He landed in Boston early in February, and after some days moved on to New York, Philadelphia, Baltimore and Washington. He talked with leading men everywhere and was surprised to find that no one questioned **the right** of South to secede if it so chose. This was true even of members of the president's cabinet. They questioned the **wisdom** of the step, but no one **denied the right** of a State to secede if it felt that its best interests demanded it — and each State must be the judge as to its own action in the premises. Moreover the textbook used at West Point when Lee was a student, was **Rawle on the Constitution**. Rawle, a distinguished Philadelphia lawyer, taught the right of secession, and that a citizen's first duty was to his own State. Hence, in withdrawing Lee was not merely following the principles imbibed with his Mother's milk, but was carrying out the instruction which the Federal Government once had given at its great War College. Surely this is not rebellion.

Perhaps a word should be inserted here as to which side was the aggressor in this historic conflict. Who bears the guilt of starting the war?

The North has sought to lay this stigma upon the South since we fired the first shot. But the courts (and common sense as well) have decreed the aggressor is not the one who strikes the first blow but the one who makes that blow necessary. The ground on which Ft. Sumter stood had been lent to the Federal Government by the State of South Carolina for the erection of a fort to guard its chief harbor, but when South Carolina withdrew from the Union, the property automatically reverted to the State. A commission was sent to Washington by the CSA to make peaceable adjustment of all matters at issue between the two governments. Chief among these was the evacuation of Ft. Sumter, then manned by Federal troops. Secretary of State Seward, speaking for the USA, gave positive assurance that he was "in favor of peace,"

and "Sumter would be evacuated in less than ten days." But it later developed that a fleet was being secretly fitted out at New York for the reinforcement of Sumter, and not until this fleet was nearing Charleston was the commission notified of this change of purpose. They at once filed an earnest protest coupled with the warning that the arrival of a hostile fleet before Sumter must be accepted by the South, and regarded by the world, as a declaration of war against the CSA. The protest was ignored, and the fleet continued on its fateful way. Then on April 12, 1861, as a defense against invasion, "the gun was fired whose sound echoed round the world." Morally and legally, the first blow was struck not at Charleston but when this fleet with hostile intent weighed anchor in the harbor of New York. Hence the guilt of aggression lies at the door of the Federal Government at Washington. (See Stephens *History of U. S.*, pp. 421-429.)

III. It is charged our Fathers fought to maintain slavery.

I have attempted to show the North fought to hold us to a partnership which had become obnoxious to its Southern members. The South fought for its simple and inalienable right to enter, continue or withdraw from such partnership as its interests might dictate. When the attempt was made to force us to remain, like all clear-thinking, liberty loving men, we fought for our right of choice. To do less would have been cringing and dishonor.

But to charge we fought to maintain slavery is to the last degree absurd.

The late well-informed Miss Mildred Rutherford of Athens, GA, states there were 200,000 slaveholders in the

Southern armies — about one man in every three. But there were 315,000 slaveholders in the Northern armies. Is it not of the very essence of absurdity to imply those thousands in Blue fought to destroy their own property — and especially so, since they could have accomplished the same result with the stroke of a pen and without shedding a drop of blood?

Except among a relatively small group of ultra fanatics, enforced abolition was not thought of. Moreover, the great Confederate Chieftain had freed his slaves long before the war began, while Grant was a slaveholder whose slaves were not freed until the Constitution had been amended in 1866. He married Miss Dent, daughter of a Southern planter of Missouri, who gave his daughter as part of her dowry five slaves which she took with her into the home of Ulysses Grant. Further, Mr. Custis, the father-in-law of General Lee was a large slave-owner. He died in 1857 making Lee his executor. In his will he provided for the liberation of all his slaves five years after his death. Hence late in 1862 Lee paused in the midst of the crushing duties connected with the preparation for a great battle to issue papers of liberation to all the Custis slaves. **It may be a slight digression but well worth while to say that Stonewall Jackson was also deeply concerned for the Negro and his spiritual welfare. He established a Sunday School in Lexington, VA, for them. On the night following the strain and stress of First Manassas he paused to write a letter to his pastor and enclosed a check for the support of the Negro Sunday School.**

We are faced, then by the absurd contention that an army led by an Emancipator was fighting to maintain slavery, while an army led by a slave-holder was fighting to destroy slavery.

Moreover if others had "played hands off" it is more than probable that slavery would eventually have been abolished by voluntary though gradual consent. For many far-sighted men with the brilliant President Patton of Princeton believed that while legally right, slavery was economically wrong — and more of a burden to the owner than to the enslaved — and urged a policy of gradual abolition. Well-known leaders provided for this in their wills. My brilliant, though somewhat eccentric kinsman, John Randolph of Roanoke, so provided in his will and set apart an ample sum to transport his freed slaves to Ohio, and to provide houses and land for them there. They met with a chilly reception and were subjected to grave threats (See Bruce's *Randolph*, Vol. II, p. 60). Richard Randolph, his brother, also freed his slaves and provided houses and lands for them a few miles from Farmville, VA. I have seen this settlement. It is known as Israel Hill.

President Lincoln's Emancipation Proclamation has been highly lauded by his admirers as the greatest "Moral Document" ever issued by a human government.

Well, it was not issued by government at all, but was the arbitrary act of the president alone — an act without the slightest authority in law.

Remember, the slaves were property — so recognized and protected by the Constitution. The president who had sworn to uphold the Constitution had no more right to take the slaves from their owners than he had to take their houses and lands without "due process of law."

Moreover it is not a moral document at all and does not even claim to be. With pathetic earnestness the president pleads for the kindly judgment of mankind, not because this is a moral act but because it is dictated by **"Military necessity."** Twice he so declares. He seeks not primarily the freedom of the slave, but to so disrupt the labor system of the South so production would largely cease, and riots and disorder would follow, for as Henry W. Grady once declared "a 100 lighted torches would have disbanded every Southern Army." But to the credit of the Negro, be it said, not one of them was lighted! The lighted torches were left to "Sherman's Bums" in their march through Georgia and Carolina, and to Sheridan and Hunter in the beautiful and stately valley of the Shenandoah.

Let us analyze it a bit and you will find that instead of an Emancipation Proclamation it is primarily a frank invitation to the South to lay down its arms. Hear it. In effect it says "If the states now in arms against the Federal Government do not lay down their arms within 100 days from this date (September 1862) then I will declare the slaves within their borders to be free." If language means anything that means "if you do lay down your arms, then you may keep your slaves". It was the outcome of the war, not the status of the Negro that concerned President Lincoln. More than this. All American slaves are not included in the terms of this proclamation, for he expressly excludes from its terms all the region around Norfolk and Hampton roads; New Orleans and all southern Louisiana to the gulf for these were by then under the muzzles of Federal gunboats. It does not include in its terms the District of Columbia or Maryland and other sections broadly included in the term — "the South." Yet there were tens of thousands of slaves in those areas. In other words this Proclamation says in effect if you own slaves in Washington, Baltimore, Norfolk, or New Orleans you may keep them; if you own slaves in Richmond, Raleigh, Columbia or Atlanta I will declare them free, if you do not come back into the Union. Thus this "great Moral Document" quickly degenerates under searching analysis into a transparent political move.

But further the man who penned this Proclamation had declared eighteen months before in the presence of ten thousand hearers gathered in front of the Capitol in Washington (I quote): "I have no purpose, directly or indirectly, to interfere with the Institution of Slavery in the States where it exists. **I believe I have no right to do so; and I have no inclination to do so.**" This is the glaring contradiction of the man who occupied the White House in the crucial days of the 60s.

IV. History records no more brilliant fight ever made in defense of home and country and constitutional rights than that of the "men who were the gray."

Ill-fed, ill-clothed. unsheltered, and often unshod, and with greatly inferior weapons, except for those captured from time to time from the enemy, yet for four tremendous years they bore the cause of the South on the points of their shining bayonets. They won victory after victory, and held at bay a powerful and determined foe — ably led. Seven commanders faced Lee in the two years and 10 months he led the gallant army of Northern Virginia. In that period his army killed, wounded and captured 262,000 of the enemy — a number more than twice as great as the total force under his own command during that period.

Of the seven officers who opposed him six were sent to the military "scrap-heap," and the seventh, Grant, was defeated more often and more signally than the others but was allowed to hold on, believing, as proved to be true, that the overwhelming weight of numbers and equipment must finally turn the scales. Probably the bloodiest battle in all history, if you consider the numbers engaged and the time involved, was at Cold Harbor, below Richmond, on June 3, 1864. At daybreak a mighty army of 113,000 leaped its breastworks and charged toward Lee's lines. The charge lasted 10 minutes — within 60 minutes the men in blue were back behind their own breastworks — but they had left 12,737 dead, wounded and prisoners behind, while Lee lost only about 500 men. (Cf. Fitzbugh Lee's *"General Lee"* p. 343)

Is it any wonder when Lord Wolseley was asked to name the five greatest generals of the English speaking race he chose: Marlborough, Wellington, Washington, Lee and Jackson? And when his questioner said, but my Lord, you don't include Grant, yet you know Grant defeated Lee. And Wolseley replied: "Can you call a general truly great who lost more men in 30 days than his adversary had?"

Yes they were never out-fought but always outnumbered; never out-generalled but simply crushed by superior and ever increasing force. Thus the tragic end came at last, and Lee, with breaking heart, but with proud head erect and unashamed, surrendered the mere skeleton of a once great and gallant army at Appomattox — 7,892 muskets to the army of perhaps 100,000 men with others within easy call.

"Furl that banner for 'tis weary,
Round its 'staff 'tis drooping dreary
Furl it, fold it, let it rest."

Just to remind you of the overwhelming odds against which our Fathers fought, and so place their courage and endurance in an even more brilliant light, let me give you a few salient facts.

The *Confederate Veteran* (long published in Nashville, TN) states:

"In the Confederate Army and Navy in four years there were 605,000 men. In the Union Army and Navy in four years there were 2,778,000 men.

In the Union Army and Navy in four years 680,000 of the above number were "mercenaries, Negroes, Germans, etc."

When we entered the World War in 1917 our government was sending across to Germany $83,000 a year in pensions. Of this sum $67,000 was for *civil war* pensions paid to aliens hired to subjugate the South. If this sum was still being sent 52 years after Appomattox, how much more must have been sent to these hirelings 10 or 15 years after the struggle ended?

One of my former students was placed in charge of teaching the illiterates at Camp Lee in World War I. At their first meeting a crowded room was asked who is this camp named for! And then what did General Lee do? When a lanky mountaineer rose and said: "He's the chap that licked the Huns the other time." When you consider the facts listed above you realize there was more truth than error in that ignorant reply.

With 75,000 more mercenaries, and many of them Germans, in the opposing force than the total enlistment in all the armies and the navy of the South, "Lee was the chap that so often licked the Huns the other time."

I have spoken with the utmost frankness, and I believe I have spoken "by the Book," that you may know assuredly your Fathers were not traitors or rebels but brave men and true, "who knew their rights and knowing dared maintain them." For loyalty is not nurtured on untruths. Patriotism is not bred by distorting or suppressing the plain facts of history. Our Fathers fought long and gallantly — and lost. We frankly accept the result without one tinge of shame or apology for them, but rather with swelling pride that in our veins flows the blood of gallant men who dared to fight for the right as God gave them to see the right. But for us — their children — there is now but one country — the good old USA. There is but one flag — the star-spangled banner. There is but one great National love: the land of the Free and the home of the Brave.

Our attitude is expressed in these simple lines whose author I do not recall:

"Here's to the Blue of, the wind-swept North
As they meet on the fields of France.
May the Spirit of Grant be with them all
As the Sons of the North advance.
And here's to the Gray of the Sun-kissed South
As they meet on the field of France,
May the spirit of Lee be with them all
As the Sons of the South advance.
And here's to the Blue and the Grey as one
As they meet on the fields of France,
May the Spirit of God be with them all
As the Sons of the Flag advance."

About the Author

Henry Tucker Graham was born on August 21, 1865, in Winchester, Virginia. He was the son of James Robert and Fanny Bland Tucker (Magill) Graham.

He had an extensive education starting with a Bachelor of Arts degree from Hampden-Sydney College in 1886, followed up with a Bachelor of Divinity, Union Theological Seminary, Richmond, Virginia, in 1891, Doctor of Divinity from Washington and Lee University in 1910 and the University of Pittsburgh in 1912.  However, he was not finished, receiving his Doctor of Laws from Hampden-Sydney College in 1934.

Rev. Graham was ordained into the Presbyterian ministry in 1891. He first served as a missionary in Japan from 1891-1896. Returning to the United States, he became a pastor in Fayetteville, North Carolina, from 1897-1904 and in Farmville, Virginia, from 1904-1908.

He left the ministry to return to his alma mater, Hampden-Sydney College, to serve as its president from 1908-1917. But he became disillusioned with the increasing cost of colleges and returned to the ministry to serve as pastor at 1st Presbyterian Church in Florence, South Carolina, from 1917-1940, when he retired.

He married Lilian Gordon Baskerville on August 12, 1891 and they had one daughter, Alice.

Graham died on January 8, 1951, and is buried in Mount Hope Cemetery in Florence, South Carolina.

Other publications from

Lincoln As The South Should Know Him
.... O.W. Blacknall

Truth of the War Conspiracy of 1861
.... H. W. Johnstone

A Story Behind Every Stone
....Charles E. Purser

As You May Never See Us Again
....Joel Craig and Sharlene Baker

Additional Information and Amendments to the North Carolina Troops 1861 – 1865 Volume I & II
....Charles E. Purser

Memoir of Nathaniel Macon of North Carolina
.... Weldon N. Edwards

Sherman's Rascals
.... Frank B. Powell, III

A Southern View of the Invasion of the Southern States and War of 1861-65
.... Captain Samuel A. Ashe

A Confederate Catechism
.... Lyon Gardiner Tyler

General Robert E. Lee
.... Captain Samuel A. Ashe

General Lee and Santa Claus
.... Louise Clack

The Life of Nathaniel Macon
.... William E. Dodd

The Land We Love — The South and It's Heritage
.... Dr. Boyd Cathey

Pickett or Pettigrew? An Historical Essay
.... Captain W. R. Bond

A View of the Constitution of the United States of America .... William Rawle

The Confederate Myth-Buster
....Walter D. Kennedy

Confederate States Military Prison at Salisbury, NC
....Dr. A. W. Mangum

More information available at
www.scuppernongpress.com

The Scuppernong Press
PO Box 1724
Wake Forest, NC 27588

www.ingramcontent.com/pod-product-compliance
Lightning Source LLC
Chambersburg PA
CBHW050337120526
44592CB00014B/2215